O, What a Luxury

GARRISON KEILLOR

O, What a Luxury

VERSES
LYRICAL, VULGAR,
PATHETIC & PROFOUND

GROVE PRESS • NEW YORK

"O What a Luxury" appeared in a slightly different form in
We Are Still Married. "Love Poem" appeared in a slightly different
form in *Wobegon Boy.*

Printed in the United States of America
Published simultaneously in Canada

ISBN 978-0-8021-2284-1
eISBN 978-0-8021-9303-2

Grove Press
an imprint of Grove/Atlantic, Inc.
154 West 14th Street
New York, NY 10011

Distributed by Publishers Group West

www.groveatlantic.com

14 15 16 17   10 9 8 7 6 5 4 3 2 1

To
Ogden Nash, Cole Porter, John Updike,
Ira Gershwin, Roger Miller, Roy Blount, Jr.
Masters of the House

CONTENTS

4 BENEATH THEIR SHINY DOMES
THEY CONTAIN YOUR CHROMOSOMES

1

WAS ETHEL MERMAN A MORMON?

UNIFICATION

The Mississippi at its mouth
Joins the Gulf of Mexico,
The west wind mixes with the south,
High pressure with the low.
Nothing in nature stands apart,
All things rendezvous—
And I would like to mingle with you.
Intermingled, intertwined,
This is what I have in mind,
A sudden urge
To merge.

The compound that is chlorophyll
Formed as the light increases
Makes every little flower thrill
With photosynthesis.
The morning glory mingles
With the honeysuckle vine.
Come wrap your little tendrils around mine.

I've been lonely as a cloud,
Drifting high and small and proud,
Lonely as a limestone butte—
Handsome, noble, destitute,
And I need you, I confess.
Let's coalesce.

BILLY THE KID

Billy the Kid
Didn't do half of what they said he did.
He rustled cattle, I guess it's true,
But bad men was who they belonged to.
He killed some guys, but if you knew 'em
You'd say they had it coming to 'em.

Billy the Kid went on the run
Down to Mesilla in 1881.
Sheriff Pat Garrett put on the heat
And came to the ranch of Billy's friend Pete
But it wasn't Billy who was shot by Pat,
It was someone wearing his pants and hat.
Billy the Kid was miles away
In Santa Fe with flowers in his hair
And I know cuz I was there.

He made a fortune in fermented juices
And built a mansion in Las Cruces,
Changed his name to William Bonney,
Wrote "Way Down Upon the Swanee"
And he may have been guilty to a degree
But he was always good to me
And generous to my family.
Always sent us a Christmas turkey
From Albuquerque
And chocolate candy
From the Rio Grande
And an embroidered pillow
From Amarillo.

I spoke at his funeral long ago.
He was living in San Luis Obispo,
Big house
On the beach.
I gave a nice speech.
People were impressed.
They didn't know he was
The most famous outlaw in the West,
Feared from Tucson to Reno.
They knew him as Rudy Valentino.

NOBODY LOVES YOU

Once I lived a life of some renown,
People looked up to me in this town.
They listened to what I had to say.
They named a sandwich for me at Bud's Café.
Then they passed a no-smoking law: no smokes, zero,
    nada.
And I became persona non grata.

Nobody loves me
When I take a smoke.
I pull out a Camel or a Lucky Strike,
They point to the door and say, "Take a hike."
I step out on the sidewalk and take my drag
With the homeless lady with the garbage bag.

I went to a party at some old pals' of mine.
They grilled steaks, poured a vintage wine.
After dinner, feeling swell
I reached in my pocket, pulled out a Pall Mall.
The room got silent, and everyone froze
Like I'd just thrown up or taken off my clothes.
I had to stand out back to indulge in my sin
Leaning up against the recycling bin.

Out on the street, the smokers stand,
Aliens in a foreign land.
Ginger Rogers smoked and so did Fred Astaire.
It was considered debonair.
Clark Gable smoked, and Cary Grant.
And nowadays you simply can't.
People don't want elegance. They want Clean Air.
So we must stand outdoors and freeze
Under the bare limbs of elm trees,
Me and Bogie and Ernie Hemingway,
Huck Finn, Woody Guthrie, Prince Andrei,
One cold day I was talking to Chopin,
Shivering, smoking a cigarette (Turkish).
Is this a decent way to treat a man
Who wrote those magnificent mazurkas?

EPISCOPALIAN
(R.I.P. Fats Waller)

I'm slow to anger, don't covet or lust.
No sins of pride except sometimes I really must.
Episcopalian, waiting around for you.

The theology's easy, the liturgy too.
Just stand up and kneel down and do what the others do.
Episcopalian, saving myself for you.

At St. Michael's, we recycle.
At St. Clements, we suck lemons.
Morning dawns on great white swans on the lawns of
    St. John's.

There's white folks and black, and gay and morose,
Some male Anglo-Saxons but we watch them pretty close.
Episcopalian, maybe you're Anglo too.

ONION SOUP

Sometimes in our lives, there is pain, there are headaches.
But what a difference homemade onion soup makes.
Boil a chicken to make bouillon
With salt and tarragon
And several chopped onions.
Simmer over a low flame.
Add carrots and celery,
And (why not?) a cup of champagne,
And more onions.
If you're depressed with phlegm in your chest,
Lonesome in winter in the Midwest,
Toss in a sliced chicken breast,
Add croutons or wonton,
Call up Leon, Diane, Don Juan,
Yvonne Dionne, William Shawn, Louis Kahn, Pope John,
   that whole group,
And serve them soup.

MORMONS

Was Ethel Merman a Mormon?
And how about Jessye Norman,
General Sherman or Uma Thurman?
Mormon? or German?

In an enormous auditorium
The former Mormons stood
Performing "Stormy Weather"
As warmly as they could.

I'm not a Mormon, nor are you,
Neither was Harmon Killebrew.
The Little Mermaid used to be.
She murmured "Mormon" once to me.

There was a New York doorman
And a dorm of sophomore men
Who adored Marilyn Monroe—
Was she a Mormon? I donno.

Are former ermine farmers Mormon?
Jorma Kaukonen, Norman Mailer
Or Popeye the Sailor?
Pee-Wee Herman or Norma Shearer?
Was there a Mormon in their mirror?

ON THE BEACH

Children walking to and fro.
Are they wearing sunscreen? No.
Babies sitting in the sand
Eating food with filthy hands.

Men who go without long pants or
Shirts are asking for skin cancer.
Naked women soon will be
In chemotherapy.

Food left sitting in the sun,
Salmonella has begun.
Young girls talking to strange men
Who just escaped from the state pen.

Why are we here at the ocean,
Under cover, drenched with lotion?
If only we had used our brains
And stayed home on the snowy plains.

THONG SONG

To people raised in a railroad shack
It is known as your butt crack.
To people who are more verbally deft
It is known as the gluteal cleft.
Either way, it's at the bottom of your back
Between the one on the right and the one on the left.

Some ladies' swimwear of slender heft
Displays freely the gluteal cleft.
On this matter, my mind is shut:
Don't walk around showing off your butt
Please desist at least
Until I am deceased.

Your gluteal cleft, I must insist,
Should be seen by your dermatologist
When treating a rash, or cyst,
And nobody else. No daughter of mine
Wears thongs. That's the bottom line.

NEWT

Newt, Newt
Wears an Extra Large suit.
His hair is shaped like a parachute.
A grand old Republican galoot
With a gleam in his eye and a smirk on his snoot
And a horn on his belt he is happy to toot.
Oh he can shimmy and he can shout:
Up with the flag, throw the scoundrels out!
Hurray for the crackers! Down with the fruit!
He's a big balloon with a very slow leak.
What you'd say for a minute, Newt can say for a week.
He knows what politics is all about.
Never had a moment's doubt.
Here's the handle, there's the spout.
Cash goes in and the steam comes out.

EPITHALAMION

After she took a pith,
I happily lay me on
Her and there with
Her, all restraint gone,
We got excited,
We passionate two O
We united
E pluribus duo.
Between the sheets,
Belly to belly,
The envy of Keats
And also of Shelley.

ON THE ROAD

I like to get behind the wheel of an automobile
And drive the 405 with a girl in the front seat
Green bikini and skin so clean and sweet
Bare feet up on the dashboard
A spoiler in back and four on the floor
Mirror shades and the radio playing hits back to back
Rat Pack, Hit the Road Jack, Mack the Knife
Tires humming on a summertime afternoon
Someday we'll get old but no time soon
Past pink bougainvillea and neon signs
And old tan people with frosted hairdos
Polyester suits and shiny white shoes
Black-leather hipsters with two-tone hair
Go ahead and stare, they don't care
Roses, lantana, jasmine in the air
Morning glory vines on the green stucco motel
A little pink pool under the palm trees
Half Hour Photo—we do video and DVDs.
No cops no stops, make a left turn on the red
And here's the Dew Drop Drive-in up ahead
Carhop walks up, I say Cokes and ice
Hamburgers, well-done, onion, bucket of fries
Baby doll you and me living free
And seeing L.A.
Sh-bop sh-bop sh-bop yeah yeah hey hey
And we'll have fun fun fun til Daddy takes the T-Bird
    away

HALE BOPP

Every four thousand years it swings on by,
A hundred twenty three million miles high,
Big and bright as a comet can be
And I feel its gravity pulling on me.
I see it in the sky at night
And my head spins and feet get light.
It's only twenty-three miles wide,
Nothing but ice and dust inside,
But on April 1st it approaches the sun,
Achieving its perihelion.
I'll dance with you and we will not stop
Until the 8th of May
When the comet fades away.
Life is short. Things disappear.
Got to catch them while they're here.
One last dance? Thank you, ma'am.
Hale Bopp a wop bop bam.

IN LOVE

Doctor, doctor, I am ill.
First I'm hot and then I'm chilled.
Heart is pounding like a pump,
Little noises make me jump.
Doctor smiled and shook his head
And said, For this, there is no cure.
You're a goner, that's for sure
Nothing helps that I know of—
You're in love.

I went to a gospel preacher.
He said, O you sinful creature,
Kneel down and repent
Right here in my gospel tent.
But a painted lady in a Cadillac
Was waiting for him out back.
Preacher, preacher, not you too?
Yes, he said, what can I do?

I cut a hole in the ice
And I walked around it twice.
Finally I jumped in
To cleanse myself of carnal sin.
And a woman with no clothes
Slowly from the water rose,
Shimmying her narrow hips
And kissed me on the lips.
I guess that's the chance you take,
Jumping in a lake.

Love is the universal sport
The night is dark and life is short
The heart is open, always willing,
The touch of skin is so fulfilling.
Darling, when I look at you
There is not much I can do.
Touch is push and push is shove—
I'm in love.

THE FABULOUS FOX

We're here at the Fabulous Fox
It dazzles it glitters it rocks
If it doesn't thrill
You then nothing will
And you should be laid out in a box.
The lobby is truly deluxe
Makes you feel you are wearing a tux
The design is Chinese but Mexican too
With touches of Aztec Egypt Peru
Some statuary for atmosphere
Greek columns and a French chandelier.
The extravagance is so ridiculous
You'd think Czar Nicholas
Was on his way
With Pope Leo, Delores Del Rio and the mayor of Pompeii.
But no it's just me and Darlene
Here to see *Halloween*
And *The Creature*
A double feature.

CHIVALRY

I would climb mountains, swim the seas,
Walk through a swarm of bumblebees,
Even jump off Lover's Leap
For Meryl Streep.

For Bonnie Raitt, I'd be braver.
If the great ship went down, I'd save her.
    Run barefoot cross the burning decks,
    Save Hillary, Angelina,
    Angela, Melina, Tina,
    Anything for the gentle sex.

If I were with Zadie Smith,
I'd write great literature,
Hoping to catch her.
I would paint the Sistine ceiling
If Christine McVie were kneeling at my feet and saying,
Please.
I'd compose symphonies,
I'd write *The Scarlet Letter*
If I could know Scarlett Johansson better.
Or an epic drama
For Michelle Obama.

ODE TO THE WOMEN ON THE MURAL AT THE STATE THEATRE, HENNEPIN AVENUE, MINNEAPOLIS

Dear naked ladies
Up in the air
Naked gurals
Of the murals
I love your hair

Here it's November
The season of flu
Weather is cold and drear
Nobody's naked here
Except for you

Had a good summer
Though it was dry
I felt mortality
Reach out for me,
Time flying by

I go to work at eight
Try to write prose
Some mornings it's good
Some I wish we could
Take off our clothes

Dear naked ladies
Your naked form
Your physiognomies
Withstand the winter freeze
Keep us all warm

Dear naked ladies
Up in the air
Ladies of my delight
Hope to rise up some night
And meet you there

KANSAS

Savannah, Santa Fe, Montana
Laurel Canyon, Susquehanna
San Francisco or Manhattan
Eat your heart out, I'm in Kansas.

I'm in Kansas,
Handsome Kansas
In the land of long romances
Fertile plants and cash finances
Handsome mansions, the advance
Of man's expansion here in Kansas.

Rembrandt, Cezanne, could've painted Kansas
The landscape's like the south of France is.
Chopin would have written dances
Had he hung his pants in Kansas.

All the saints, including Francis,
Prayed that if the Good Lord grants us
Second chances, could we
Transubstantiate to Kansas?

UROLOGY

Urology Urology
O tell me what's the matter
At the pot I try to pee
It trickles out erratically
And then it leaks all over me
I have a sad old bladder.

Urology Urology
When working on my plumbing
Be careful where you put your knife
I have to entertain my wife
She beats the drum. I play the fife.
I love to hear her coming.

SHOW BUSINESS

Life is like a circus parade
Marching along as the calliope's played.
There you are, young and elegant,
Up on the back of the lead elephant
In your glittery costume
And I'm the guy with the shovel and broom.
My assignment is to scoop
Up the piles of elephant poop.
You, my love, are youth and beauty.
I'm on sanitation duty.
A slight demotion, yes, I know
But I'm still with the show,
Enjoying the hullabaloo
And the health benefits are okay too,
Same as if I were a star,
So there you are.

DOXOLOGY

O Lord, please bless our old State Fair,
The riders whirling in the air,
The ladies who have baked the pies
Competing for the First Grand Prize.

Praise God from whom all blessings flow,
The rodeo and talent show.
Praise Him for sugar and for grease,
And may He grant our stomachs peace.

The 4-H girls who show their llamas,
Weeping infants and their mamas,
The homely girl in the homemade dress,
The lonely ones, dear Lord, please bless.

Forgive our gluttony and noise.
Protect the Demolition Derby boys.
May the Fat Man still be sweet
Despite the gawkers at his feet.

PSALM

Blessed is the man who does not sit in the seat of the
scornful. But his delight is in the LORD.

O give thanks unto the LORD; for He is good: for
His mercy endureth for ever even through the 2012
presidential campaign.

Yea, though Barack Obama went blank during the first
debate and let that gilded idiot Romney smarm and
strut and puff, yet will I give thanks unto Thee, O
LORD GOD.

Yea, though the Gallup poll shows the race in a dead
heat and Romney is full of crazed confidence,
and we must contemplate the return of Calvinist
economics and smallpox and indentured servitude
and stiffer sentences for stealing bread, yet will I
praise Thee, O LORD GOD.

And though it is late October, and my tongue bleeds
from biting it when people whom I know personally
say that maybe Romney can get the economy
moving, yet I will attempt to praise the LORD for
His goodness to me.

Romney will be elected President and the White House
will be full of grinning Caucasoids who believe God
has given them dominion over the earth. Have mercy
upon me and answer me, O LORD.

And the LORD hath shown mercy. Barack Obama won
Wisconsin, Michigan, Pennsylvania, Ohio, Virginia,
Nevada, and Florida, and Mr. Romney came on TV
stunned, tongue-tied, and the Koch Brothers and
Karl Rove were confounded and had to eat their
underwear and Mr. Obama gave an elegant victory
speech and we went to bed saying, Thanks be to
You, O LORD. Your mercy endureth forever. Amen.

2

A MAJOR FAUX PAS PROHIBITED BY LAW

O, WHAT A LUXURY

O, what a luxury it be
What pleasure O what perfect bliss
So ordinary and yet chic
To pee to piss to take a leak

To feel your bladder just go free
And open like the Mighty Miss
And all your cares go down the creek
To pee to piss to take a leak

For gentlemen of great physique
Who can hold water for one week
For ladies who one quarter-cup
Of tea can fill completely up
For folks in urinalysis
For little kids just learning this
For Viennese or Swiss or Greek
For everyone it's pretty great
To urinate

Women are quite circumspect
But men can piss with great effect
With terrible hydraulic force
Can make a stream or change its course
Can put out fires or cigarettes
And sometimes laying down our bets
Late at night outside the bars
We like to aim up at the stars

O yes for men it's much more grand
Women sit or squat
We stand
And hold the fellow in our hand
And proudly watch the golden arc
Adjust the range and make our mark
On stones and posts for rival men
To smell and not come back again

A QUESTION

His wife said, "Please be careful," and he smiled patiently
And said, "Hey, don't worry about me."
And he buckled right in with a confident grin
And his screwdriver touched a live wire.
And he let out a cry and proceeded to die
In a shower of sparks and fire.
And the people who gave the eulogy
Spoke of honor and love and ambition.
They spoke well of the dead, and nobody said,
"Why didn't he call an electrician?"

MANNERS

1.
Mind your manners at all times and places.
Be polite on a regular basis.
Say *Buenos días* as someone approaches,
Or, if it's evening, say *Buenas noches*,
And please try not to stare.
Everyone has their burden to bear,
So don't be rude.
The man with a snake around his neck
And platform shoes and birdcage hair,
Yes, he does appear to be nude—
But what the heck?
Everyone is somewhat unique.
One man's normal is another man's freak.
No matter where you're from,
You too may stick out like a sore thumb.
Yes, that lady's neckline is low,
But you've seen breasts before, I know,
And unless you're an infant who needs to be fed,
Put your eyes back in your head.

2.

Good manners! What more can I say?
Please and *Thank you* go a long way.
Excuse me and *After you* and *If I may.*
Always chew with your mouth shut
And please don't scratch your butt.
Do Swedes or Norwegians
Scratch their nether regions?
Did President Bush
Reach back and itch his executive tush?
No. Only savage brutes
Digitally address their glutes.
Someday you may be distinguished
And give a speech in very good English
At Harvard, to heavy applause,
And because
You feel a low irritation—
There is a temptation,
But please. Where were you raised?
In a home of good taste
Or in a little mud hut?
Don't scratch your butt.

3.
A fine young man on his way to a meeting,
Handsome, well-dressed, with a beard,
Across the parking lot was proceeding,
When suddenly his finger disappeared.

I thought, *Please don't pick your nose.*
No matter how good it feels.
Doing it out in the open shows
You're an oaf and a lummox. Even CEOs
Behind smoked glass in automobiles
Who suffer from social psychosis
Don't pick their noses.
Do and your stock will drop
And that beautiful woman will cry, "Please stop!"
And she'll go away and she will not miss you.
Use a tissue.

AT THE GRAMMYS

I went to the Grammys to accept an award,
Dressed in a tux I could ill afford,
Surrounded by women in such low-cut gowns
I looked in their eyes and did not dare look down.

I sat in the third row, a seat on the aisle,
And smiled a modest but generous smile,
And thought of my speech and of whom to include
In a long litany of false gratitude.

The emcee came out with a big envelope
And said how excited he was (the big dope),
And opened it, pulled out the paper, from which
He read the name of that son of a bitch,

A pretentious ignorant total nitwit
Whose body of work is a pile of shit.
He hugged his wife and feigned joyful confusion.
And I wished he'd have a cerebral occlusion.

He said he was lucky, he dabbed at a tear—
His self-deprecation was so insincere.
He thanked his wife and his dear family,
And his producer, and then he thanked me.

He called me a genius, and called for a hand
And so I was forced to smile and stand
And wave and acknowledge the honor and all.
I wished I could gouge out his left eyeball.

I tore out of there fast, back to my hotel,
Didn't answer the phone or the doorbell.
In the morning I looked at the paper and read
He'd been found at midnight, dead in his bed.
I felt guilty for the thoughts I had thought
But I went to his funeral—why not?
My eulogy sounded completely sincere
And I won the Grammy the very next year.

FREQUENT FLYER

You are waiting at the gate
For a flight two hours late.
The clerks are rude
And your seat is in back.
And the A/C isn't working
And the overheads are packed.

It's a middle seat, two feet wide,
Two large people on either side.
And the seat ahead of you
Leans back in your lap
And your knees are gently fractured
And you feel your backbone snap.

Lunch will be pretzels and Coke
And your neighbors are chatty folk.
They ask where you're going
And what you're going for.
You sit with your eyes closed
And pretend to snore.

Like a prisoner in the stocks,
Like a body in a box,
You feel uneasy
As the plane begins to shake,
And you wonder if this trip
Will be your tragic last mistake.

Do not think of flying
Into the ground and dying,
Think about when you retire
To that cottage on the shore
To become a kindly recluse
Who never sets foot out his door.

You will lie in your bed,
Hearing engines overhead.
Think how happy you will be,
In fact overjoyed.
And all your smoke detectors
Disabled or destroyed.

WINTER GUESTS

In autumn when the days get short,
The mice move into the davenport
And settle in with great esprit
Deep in the upholstery.
Tiny bug and rodent friends
Come to share your residence.
Bats and squirrels and raccoons too
Quietly move in with you.
Try as you will to fill the cracks,
Set traps, mount poison gas attacks,
In the face of winter weather
Creatures like to join together.
So don't cry out in shock and fright
If a badger comes to supper tonight.
Or a possum. Possums are polite.
They'd like a salad and crème brûlée
And a chamomile tea and then go away.
Deer are well-spoken as everyone knows.
No *dese* or *dem* for the well-bred does.
Though you should be careful with bison.
They are all very nice in
A pasture or stable,
But seat them at your dining room table,
And you will see they bolt their food,
Their table talk is very rude,
And they do not ever use a commode,
They just sit and drop a buffaload.

AMAZON

I'm getting tired of the northern hemisphere,
Tired of the cold on the prairie.
In all my dreams I think of Peru,
Where summer falls in January.
I miss that old rain forest,
The snakes and cockatoos.
Miss the Amazon and you.

Put away my parka, put my pajamas on.
I'm heading back to my home on the Amazon,
My house, my home, *mi casa.*
Home of the nova and the bossa.
Miss those corn tortillas,
Miss the sweet guitars
Miss the *Buenos días*
Miss tequila bars—
Why am I in Minnesota
Stead of in old Peru?
Miss the Amazon and you.

LETHARGY

I should be writing my memoir.
In March it's due.
Instead I'm in Miami,
Lying in the sun with you.

Hand me the suntan lotion,
Pass me a lemon fizz.
Don't give me that newspaper, babes
Don't tell me what day it is.

I could've been a contender,
A winner, a leading man.
Instead I'm in Miami,
A bum with a suntan.

The memoir's about my struggle
Up from poverty.
Here I am at the Biltmore,
Stuck on page 23.

Ladybug in the left margin
And the line she's creeping by:
"Lying in the hospital,
Thinking Mom would die,
I promised myself if she survived
I would bid gin goodbye."
Ladybug looks at it and laughs.
It's a lie, whole thing is a lie.

OCEAN CROSSING

On the Queen Mary 2
Everything that can be done for you
Is done. You are well-fed
From a long menu
And you sleep on a lovely bed
Under a feathery duvet.
All day
You lie in the sun dreamily
Sipping fresh lemonade
Or in the shade
With a cup of tea,
Gazing at the Atlantic,
Passing smoothly over the wreck of the *Titanic,*
The ice in the lemonade clinking
As you avoid thinking about sinking
Suddenly into the sea,
Nearer my God to Thee.
A peaceful sunny day
And God is very far away
And there is no need for the lifeboats to be lowered
In hysteria
As the ship begins its plunge.
Forward!
To the cafeteria!
Let's have lunch.

3

I LIVE IN
THIS DESOLATE SPOT
BECAUSE YOU DO NOT

SEATTLE

Everything is uphill in Seattle.
Everywhere you go, you have to climb.
Everything is an uphill battle
If you want to get there on time.

> *Excuse me, where is the Capital Grille?*
> It's six blocks up that hill.

People do not coast in this town.
They don't believe in the fall of man.
They're never depressed, or feel let down.
If you're tired you can move to Spokane.
Maybe it's the fresh salt air,
Maybe it's the coffee in your cup.
You climb the hill and there is a stair
And it goes up.

Pedaling with powerful thighs
On their upward routes
Seattleites trying to rise
And get above the clouds.
They bike, they hike, they race
Up that long incline.
They're heading for a place
Where there is sunshine.

Excuse me. I'm looking for heaven.
It's straight ahead. Six blocks or seven.
No sorrow, and we'll never be ill?
It's right up that hill.

SAN FRANCISCO

A foggy January day in Golden Gate Park, blessed and
   beatific,
Sixty-two degrees under the eucalyptus trees beside the
   Pacific,
The fragrance of cypress and Monterey pine, magnolia
   in bloom
Giving off magnolia perfume,
And cherry blossoms and lotuses, or lota.
A teenage couple making out in a Chinese pagoda
Who stop suddenly as Asian grannies walk in,
Talking high-speed Mandarin.

An old man does tai chi by the sidewalk
By Stow Lake with rowboats lined up by the dock.
Turtles sitting on rocks in the sun.
Old ladies on a bench, knitting, every one.
Strawberry Hill, a steep climb to a view of the city and
   its hills
And clouds like fields of white daffodils.
A view that awakens the senses like a cosmic reveille
Though you are breathing heavily.
And you turn and see on the western horizon—
Could it be? It can't. But it is. Bison.
Several of them, grazing in a field, and beyond, the
   setting sun
Like a pink and orange vision
Of pure joy,

No wonder people from Indiana, Ohio, North Dakota,
    and Illinois
Come here to awaken their old romance
In a park of flowering plants
Under a Pacific sky,
How could one not be in love, even if you're not sure
    with whom or why?

L.A.

On a summer day in a cool car
Driving with the top down on Sunset Boulevard,
Yellow light speed up, turn on the red, stay in motion
From downtown 22 miles out to the ocean,
Past Sunset & Gower, and the old Columbia studio,
Home of Frank Capra, and Curly, Larry and Moe,
And here is the gate they used to walk through:
Nyuk nyuk nyuk. Woo woo woo.
Past the Roosevelt Hotel and Hollywood High,
And a lady with pin-up hair and penciled brow over
     each eye.
The Hollywood Palladium, and at Sunset & Vine
You look up and see the Hollywood sign.
In-N-Out Burger, Tarot reading, strip club *Girls Girls Girls.*
A liquor store with a neon sign that flashes as it twirls.
And beyond the neon signs and the gin mills
The sculpted hedges of Beverly Hills
And houses like reinforced stockades
In Bel Air and Pacific Palisades.
Then the Pacific Coast Highway and you end your run
At the edge of the water looking at the setting sun.
And what more is there to say?
You've come to the end. Roll the credits. L.A.

TIMES SQUARE

I was born with an affliction,
A disposition or mood
Of silent introspection,
A tendency to brood.
I brood about good people I knew
In the bygone time gone by
& what I should've done & didn't do
& won't before I die.

But I come to New York (*boom boom*)
& the razzmatazz, hullabaloo & jazz.
>The guy with a snake wound around his chest
>The anti-fur protest
>A street-corner preacher and the quack quack man
>Boys beating on a garbage can
>The river of taxis and the quiet roar
>Of ambition. And I don't feel sorry anymore.
Henry Thoreau went to Walden Pond,
Sat at a table in a straightback chair.
I'd rather be in Times Square
& look at that six-story blonde
On the billboard wearing black underwear.
>And a lady out of a fashion magazine
>A lady in black, her lips bright red
>How did she ever get into those jeans
>A beautiful woman, so I'll just drop dead
>New York—(*boom boom*) when all is said
>Is where I go to get out of my head.

KATZ'S

From Times Square, the F train takes you to the Lower
    East Side
To East Houston and Delancey, to be satisfied
At Katz's Deli, the name in red letters: K-A-T-Z-
    APOSTROPHE-S.
A monument to fidelity in a maze of temporariness.
All around are punk bars and hipster dives
Where Jews in tenements like beehives
Believed that if they were true to each other and the Lord,
Their children would reap a great reward.
It is vanished, the land of Yiddish,
And we Americans are skittish
As waterbugs, but Katz's,
For Republicans, Socialists, Anarchists, or Democrats, is
A beacon of corned beef and pastrami,
As permanent as Leviticus or Deuterami.
And delicious knishes.
The synagogue is a theater now. The whole street is a play.
A man in a yellow skirt and leather boots in a doorway
Waits for someone and next
To him, teen girls stand and text.
A dude with sideswept bangs
And skinny tie hangs
With a lady in leather with a face tattoo and lip ring,
Nuzzling and nickering
Ten feet from Katz's Delicatessen
Which offers chicken soup and a lesson

In true love and what true means:
Which is that one can feast on frankfurters and beans
If the one who shares your booth
Is true to you. And that's the truth.

CITY LIFE

There was once a sensitive young man who left his
    country home
And moved to the city to be more free
For in the city people considered sensitivity a sign of
    intelligence
Whereas in the country they considered it a pain in the
    neck.

So he got a nice apartment and a job as a clerk in a
    bookstore
And he purchased several outfits, all of which were
    black.
And he went to smart cafes where he always sat in the
    corner
Where the light was dim, which made him appear
    mysterious.

He enjoyed his city life and stayed out late at night
And went to shows they did not have in Granite Falls
And the only thing that troubled him was what if he
    got sick
And fell down in the street, would anyone notice?

He decided to find out and he lay down in the gutter
And right away someone knelt down by his side
And it was his old neighbor from Granite Falls who
    had come to the city to visit her niece Denise
And she said, "Jim, I always knew you would wind up
    this way."

READER

Holly Golightly takes a taxi down to Tiffany's
As Holden Caulfield walks west in a hurry.
She is calmed by the sight of diamond jewelry
And he by the solidity of the Museum of Natural
    History.

And A. J. Liebling walks along 43rd toward Times
    Square,
One o'clock in the morning and all the tourists are
    gone.
He stops at his watering hole and if there are no friends
    there
He makes some new ones. "A wonderful, grand old
    Babylon."

Christmas lights in the windows of brownstones,
O. Henry's story lingering there.
Jim pawned his watch to buy Della combs,
To buy him the watch chain, she sold her hair.

Jay Gatsby walks to the end of his great yard,
Leaving the party, the band, the dancers going round
    and round
And looks at the green light out there in the dark,
A distant dock across Long Island Sound.

Men in fresh suits, white shirts, and ties, and wearing
    hats
Come striding out of Grand Central Station,
Salesmen, CEOs, with the hearts of Renaissance
    aristocrats,
Direct from John Cheever's rich imagination.

On the 17th floor Sylvia Plath in her summer dress
Stands at the window and smells the city's mysteries,
E. B. White said: New York bestows the gift of
    loneliness.
No one should come to live here unless willing to be
    lucky.

And so in New York, I feel at ease
In crowds of strangers hereamong,
From the East 20s to the West 70s,
Walking through books I read when I was young.

LIMERICKS: NEW YORK

There was a young man of Park Slope
Who liked to be tied up with rope
And forced on his knees
To eat black-eyed peas
Which was good for his health, one would hope.

There was a young lady of Queens
Who survived, though of moderate means,
By riding the bus,
Shopping Army surplus,
And stealing from vending machines.

A man of the Upper West Side
Never left, he was so satisfied,
Til at age thirty-five
He went for a drive
To Vermont, caught pneumonia, and died.

There was a young man of the Bronx
Who was tired of beeps, toots, and honks,
So he went to Surrey
Where they're not in a hurry
And say Thanks, which they pronounce Thonx.

A lady who lived in Tribeca
Said, "New York is heaven! A mecca!
Though sometimes I long
For a chickadee's song,
Or the sound of a tufted woodpecca."

A poet who lived in Astoria
Wrote poems so inflammatory, a
Sonnet caught fire,
Days later, a choir
Sang Sanctus, Benedictus, and Gloria.

A sneaky old man of Wall Street
Is a liar, a crook, and a cheat.
On buses he's ridden, he's
Stolen folks' kidneys
And also the shoes off their feet.

PAPA AND HIS BABY
SEE MANHATTAN

Hush, little baby, don't say a word.
Papa's gonna take you to West 43rd,
The street where Benchley and Harold Ross
And Dorothy Parker hit the sauce
As the copy editors hit the caffeine
And put out *The New Yorker* magazine.
If literary history is not an inspiration,
Papa will take you to Grand Central Station
And if the Oyster Bar is fresh out of oysters,
We'll take the subway up to the Cloisters,
And if the tapestries do not please,
Papa will take you to Tiffany's
And if the diamonds don't glitter like they oughta,
Papa will take you to *La Traviata*
And if the Violetta does not sing prettily,
Papa will take you to Little Italy
And if the pasta's too soft and the wine's too dry,
I'll take you to the 92nd Street Y
And if the poetry reading's a bore
And the metaphors you've heard before
And the poet's muse is a much too solemn muse,
Papa's gonna take you to St. Bartholomew's
And if the pews don't give enough knee room,
Papa's gonna take you to the Russian Tea Room
And if that scene is too serene,
We'll stop in at Picholine
And if the poached perch paté pales,
Papa will take you to Bloomingdale's

And if Bloomingdale's doesn't quite bloom,
We'll head west and visit Grant's Tomb
And if his tomb fills you with gloom,
I'll take you up to the Rainbow Room
And if the Rainbow makes you blue,
We'll stop and see the Central Park Zoo
And if those polar bears are in a coma,
We'll go to an exhibition at MoMA
And if art is not what you had in mind,
We'll head west and see what we find.
Ninth Avenue in the 50s is lined
With joints where one can be wined and dined
And there Papa's credit card will be declined.
His American Express is expressionless.
He's been deVisaed and unMastered,
All because of you, you beautiful child.
Then we'll pack our bags and head for home
Out on the range where the buffalo roam,
Back to the farm, to pay our debts
And live on Cheez Whiz and Creamettes.
We'll slop the hogs and milk the cows
And take in boarders at our house,
Drive a school bus, mow the lawns,
Dig the ditches, clean the johns,
And eventually when the money's made,
And the pigs are sold and the bills are paid,
We'll put down the shovel and the pitchfork,
And get dressed up and come back to New York.

MINNESOTA ROUSER

Let winter come and walk roughshod
With sleet and freezing rains.
We fear it not, we trust in God
And jumper cables and tire chains.

We're prepared for the good fight,
We shall be cheerful though the blizzard blows.
Though it is ten below, a long cold night,
We trust in coffee and warm clothes.

From Worthington to Grand Marais,
From Lake Vermilion to Red Wing,
We thank God for the coldest day
And offer up our suffering.

From Bemidji to Anoka,
From Rochester to Roseau,
Winter makes us finer folk, a-
Las we're modest and can't say so.

CASE STUDIES

She lived in New York City,
And Melissa was her name.
Intelligent and pretty
And her life untouched by shame.
But she felt less whole, less female,
Her true self unexpressed,
So she sent her mom an e-mail,
"I have left for the Midwest."

"I've gone to Minnesota
To discover what life means,
A state where people know to
Wear long johns beneath their jeans.
I'll miss you, darling mother,
And try to write or call,
But I'm bound to seek fulfilment in the city of St. Paul."

He was a prince of Wall Street
In a long black automobile,
In a town where you see the false treat-
Ed as if it were real.
Although wildly successful
As a man of many hats,
He found it rather stressful
Trying to race with younger rats.

So he went to Minnesota
To discover what life means
A place where people gota
Get away from limousines.
Where you thrill to every sunrise
And you hark to nature's call
And finally see the light in the city of St. Paul.

A strict old Presbyterian,
Said, "Why am I so dull?
Why can't one be merry in
One's heart and soul and skull?
Why follow what John Knox taught
That life is a stone wall?
I'd rather do the fox-trot
So I'm heading for St. Paul."

He went to Minnesota
To find out what life means.
Where we all consume our quota
Of cereal and greens.
Goodbye Calvinism,
And minds that are too small.
A brighter day has risen in the city of St. Paul.

She lived in San Francisco
In the cool Pacific mists
Where she danced all night to disco
With the other hedonists.
A life of ease and sushi
And yet she felt—depressed.
And one afternoon at two she
Took a plane to the Midwest.

She left for Minnesota
And followed the North Star
And bought a farm and wrote a
Very meaningful memoir
Full of visionary
Zeal and unity and all
The beauties of the prairie and the city of St. Paul.

MINNESOTA

In the state of Minnesota, it's always warm and breezy,
And the price of soybeans rises and the hens lay eggs
  over easy.
And the children are above average
And the cops are nice, as everyone knows,
And there are no flies or mosquitoes,
And we blow our troubles away like bubbles.
There are 13,000 lakes and the grass is green
And people are honest and say what they mean.
And, yes, it's cold but the cold is *dry*
And the winter sky is a clear blue sky
And we seldom get the winter blues
And everyone has high IQs
And illiteracy we have much less of because politicians
  are all progressive
In the state of Minnesota.

O the buzzin' of the flies on the rhubarb pies and the
  alfalfa soda
You can hear the loons singing opera tunes
In the state of Minnesota.

WHY I LIVE IN MINNESOTA

Where the temp gets down to thirty below
And it's perfectly flat, miles of snow,
And you ask why I live in this desolate spot.
Why? Because you do not.

You in loud clothes
With lacquered hair
And monster pickups
And not much upstairs,
Who whoop in church
And worship the Word,
For whom evolution
Has not yet occurred.
The men shoot gators
Out in the marsh,
While the women stay home
And hang up the warsh.
It's all about rifles
And the Second Comin'
And wave the flag
And down with Gummint
And up with football
And the G.O.P.
Now what if those people
Lived next door to me?

And the only thing
That keeps them away
Is the fact it will hit
Minus thirty today?
Winter's a challenge
But it can be faced
When you're among people
With brains and good taste.

THAT'S ME

I'm a minimalist from Minnesota,
Don't waste my time and I won't waste yours.
You are the woman I love, of course.
I'm crazy about you and always have been.
And don't make me say it again.
Cause I'm a minimalist from Minnesota,
A man of monumental brevity.
That's me.

A TRUE STORY

In February three years ago
On a bitter freezing day
We packed the beer and cooler in the trunk,
For Bemidji bore away.

We launched the boat at half past noon
Though the lake was choked with ice.
The temperature was forty-five below
But we did not think twice.

We had a gallon of peppermint schnapps
And a case of Miller Lite.
We took no poles or lines or bait
For we fish with dynamite.

We lit the fuse and threw it in
And waited for the ice to burst
And we waited awhile, then Jimmy cried, "Oh no,
That was four pounds of bratwurst."

Our spirits fell as our lunch went down
And sank of its own weight,
Then the waters boiled as a hundred walleyes
Went for the bratwurst bait.

A hundred fish leaped out of the water
And we grabbed them with our hands
And filled our bucket and we filled up our boat
And we stuffed them in our pants.

And Jimmy opened a can of beer
To celebrate the catch,
And he reached in his pocket for a big cigar
And I saw him light the match.

The cigar blew Jimmy into East Grand Forks
And me into Duluth,
And since my life was spared that day
I've resolved to tell the truth.

PLUMBER

When the ice comes and the snow and it's 48 below
And then the temperature starts to fall
And they hear the moan and whine of that frozen
    water line
Then the plumber is the man who saves them all.
He is not sleek and slim and they may look down on him
But the plumber is the man who saves them all.

When the toilet will not flush and the odor makes you
    blush
And you cannot use the sink or shower stall,
Then your learning and your art slowly start to fall apart
But the plumber is the man who saves it all.
They can take their sins to Jesus but when their water
    freezes
Then the plumber is the man who saves them all.

In the innocence of youth, beauty, justice, truth,
Seem to be what life is all about,
But when the facts are faced, you realize life is based
On water coming in and going out.
It is fine to love Chopin, but when it hits the fan
The plumber is the man who saves them all.

BUS CHILDREN

Out on the prairie so wide
The school buses wending their way
From the towns they travel
For miles on the gravel
An hour before it is day.
And the winter wind blows
Cross the corn stubble rows
Where the dirt has turned the snow gray.

And the children walk down to the road
From the farmhouses' warm kitchen glow,
Stand waiting and yearning
To see the bus turning
And the sweep of the headlights' glow.
And they climb up inside
And away they all ride
Past the farms and the fields full of snow.

And they think about math as they go
And the chemistry of atmosphere
And unequal equations
And French conjugations
And the sonnets of William Shakespeare.
And then up the drive
At the school they arrive
On the darkest day of the year.

And in due course they will fly
Away, young women and men
With mixed emotions
Cross mountains and oceans
And become what we could not have been.
We will tenderly kiss them
Goodbye and miss them
And seldom will see them again.

EAU CLAIRE

Men who care for children are rare
And he's the only living house dad in Eau Claire.
His wife works and he's the au pair.
A man in a flock of moms, rather odd.
Dozens of Sarahs and just one Todd.
The mothers do not talk to him at all
At the ballet class, sitting out in the hall.
They treat him like dirt,
Like a likely pervert.
If he were in San Francisco, there'd be a House Dad
    Association
To offer mutual validation,
The latest about teeth and nutrition,
And that great museum down in the Mission,
Birthday parties and where to find magicians
And the merits of various pediatricians.
In San Francisco, a house dad is a hero.
In Eau Claire, a big zero.

He drives the kids to music lessons and sits in the car,
Working on his memoir.
It's humorous but with a slight undercurrent of despair.
It's called The Only Living House Dad in Eau Claire.

T. S. ELIOT ROCK

Let's go to St. Louis, baby, you and I
Where Mr. Chuck Berry is spread out against the sky
And the skirts trail along the floor—
Just a half a mile from the Mississippi shore.

Let's go through half-deserted streets to a one-night
    cheap hotel
Where he plays his guitar just like ringing a bell
In the room the women come and go
And I'm just a lucky so-and-so.

The night was young and the moon was gold.
I was eating a peach with my trousers rolled.
I had no particular place to go.
Hail, hail Michelangelo.

I have heard the mermaids singing, way out in the blue,
They're back to doing the things they used to do
I've known those women, I have known them all;
I do not know the number but I know who placed the
    call.

ELEGIAC

I was walking around back where I come from
In Anytown U.S.A.
And turned left and found I'd come
To Anytown Au Lait.

It's a neighborhood of lovely homes,
Retro but brand-new.
Where kids all have Celtic names
And the women are size 2.

The hair salon is The Barbary,
The butcher shop is The Carvery,
The stationery store is The Papery,
And the clerks are sales *associates*
And part of the Gap family.

Everything is handcrafted and organic,
Sustainable, nonfat, and gluten-free.
And even the shampoo is botanic
And aloe is used extensively.

I miss the graffiti on the wall
And the old galoots smoking cheroots
And the junkyard and the old pool hall
With the dudes in pinch-back suits.

I miss disreputable guys
Who lurked in a doorway.
I miss having to memorize
The chief exports of Norway.

Mostly, I miss you and me
Parked in a 1956 Pontiac
And you looking around apprehensively
As I unsnapped your bra strap in back.

PERVERSITY

A cloudy sky, I say it's blue.
Slap my face, I say "Thank you!"
You say tomato, I say tomota,
I learned it up in Minnesota.
Perversity:
It's been good to me.
The woods are lonely, dark, and gray
And all the birds have flown away.
November. Winter's almost here,
Along the road I see dead deer.
Why be sad just because it's not summer?
Don't have to march to that summer drummer
In that sunshine column.
Old man doesn't have to be solemn.
I am seventy years old.
The forecast is for snow and cold.
Things go from bad to worse
Except if you're perverse.
Let's rock and roll,
Heart and soul.

HOME ON THE PLAINS

Way out in the West where nature is blessed
With a beauty so vast and austere,
Though you have flown off to cities unknown,
Your memories bring you back here.

Home, home on the plains,
Here in the grass we will lie
When our day's work is done we will lie in the sun
As it sets in the big western sky.

Take a leisurely journey across the Missouri
And discover the brown solitude
In the great quiet land by the river Cheyenne
Where once the Mandan canoed.

Where the teepees were raised in a cool shady place
By the rivers where sweet grasses grew,
Where the bison was found on the great hunting ground
And fed all the nations of Sioux.

The canyons and buttes like old twisted roots
In the sandstone of ancient stream beds—
In the sunset they rise to dazzle our eyes
With their lavenders, yellows, and reds.

Here Crazy Horse dwells in the Black Hills,
You can hear him at night as he sings.
He was brought to his knees but he's waiting to see
What the next millennium brings.

When it comes my time to leave this world behind
And sail off to regions unknown,
May they lay my remains out on the plains
Deep in that sweet prairie home.

4

BENEATH THEIR SHINY DOMES THEY CONTAIN YOUR CHROMOSOMES

LOVE YOU DEAR

The evening sun goes down,
The midnight train is whining low
Sliding through the wrong side of town
On its way to I-Don't-Know.
But a man with a woman feels no pain.
He can dance up a wall, sing in the rain.
Hand in hand around the square
I don't wish I was anywhere
Except right here, the happiness
Of you in your long black dress,
My hand around your waist.
Let's go over to Andy's Place,
That lowdown honky-tonk.
No Chablis or Sauvignon Blanc
But I'm good for a pitcher of beer.
We'll find a corner and disappear
And kiss and neck a little, hey?
Good times are on the way.

SLOW DAYS OF SUMMER

Slow days of summer
In this old town.
Sun goes across the sky,
Sometimes a car goes by.
There's one right now.

Looks like a Chevy.
Your Chev is blue.
This Chev is white and brown,
It isn't slowing down,
Guess it's not you.

You said you'd be here
Sunday or so.
Maybe by Saturday
If you could get away,
You didn't know.

I love you, darling,
Waiting alone.
Waiting for you to show,
Wishing you'd call me though
I don't have a phone.

Waiting for love to come,
All is alive.
Birds sing in angel tongues,
Small stones like diamonds
All down the drive.

Visions of love appear,
Clouds passing through.
All of my life I see
Passing so beautifully,
Waiting for you.

Around the corner,
An old dog appears,
Stands in the summer sun
Waiting for love to come.
Wish you were here.

LOVE POEM

Here on a warm night in the grass and dry leaf smell,
Listening to crickets under the starry sky,
What lovely stories we could tell
With only these clear lights to tell them by.

A warm night, and you, and paradise,
So tender and so full of grace.
Above your head, the universe has hung its lights,
And I reach out my hand to touch your face.

I believe in impulse, in all that is green,
Believe in the faithful vision that comes true,
Believe that all that is essential is unseen,
And for this lifetime I believe in you.

    All of the lovers and the love they made:
    Nothing that was between them was a mistake.
    All that we did for love's sake
    Was not wasted and will never fade.

All who have loved shall be forever young
And walk in grandeur on a summer night
Along the avenue,
They live in every song that is sung,
In every painting of pure light,
In every pas de deux.
Love that shines from every star,
Love reflected in the silver moon.
It is not here, but it's not far.
Not yet, but it will be here soon.

THE FRONT SEAT

I fell in love in the front seat of a '56 Ford
At a drive-in movie, sliding over toward
A girl in shorts and necking a little
On a bench seat, no gearshift in the middle.

She was young and eager—it didn't take much
To slip her in gear and let out the clutch
But the beautiful bench where we performed our feats
Has been replaced by two bucket seats

And a brake lever, gearshift, and armrest
Between me and the girl I love best,
Which is sensible and safer, perhaps,
Two people restrained by safety straps,

But if safety were all that people thought of
Then who would ever fall in love?

WEDDING MARCH
FROM *LOHENGRIN*

HER: Why am I here?
Who is this man?
Why is he dressed up and holding my hand?

He's the wrong guy
He's not the one
Pick up your dress, turn around, girl, and run.

HIM: Why does she cry?
I wish she'd stop.
I'm not bad looking and I have a job.
I'm not a jerk.
Sober, I swear.
Height-weight proportionate and have my own hair.

HER: Guess it's too late, the song's almost done
Could have done better but he is the one.
I'll face the music and do as I'm able
To spend forty years across the dinner table.

ALL:
It's not so bad
It could be worse
It's better than coming to church in a hearse.

Just say the words
That must be said
And afterward you can go off to bed.

WEDDING RECESSIONAL

Here comes the bride and groom
Make room, out of the way, clear the decks.
We're going to cut the cake
And then hit the road and have sex.
We're taking off these clothes
And we'll have a glass of wine
And we'll jump between the sheets
And we will intertwine.
We'll do it fifteen times
And then tomorrow fifteen more
And we'll do it on and on
Until we're stiff and sore.
So here comes the bride and groom
We're walking fast and that's why
We're going to have some sex
So thanks for the gifts and goodbye.

CICADAS

The seventeen-year cicada crawls out of the ground
And looks around
From a wall or a low-hanging limb—
He looks for her and she discovers him.
Courtship does not extend for months.
Their only job is to have sex once.
No long interlude of pleasant reminiscing about days
    gone by.
Just buzz and whir and thank you sir and then you die.
Cicada love does not involve poetry or song.
Was it good for you? *Thanks.* So long.

FATHERHOOD

Human sperm are very small.
Five microns, that's about all,
Just a cell with a dangly tail,
A fraction of the ovum
But still you've got to love 'em
And they're produced in the testes of the male.
Beneath their shiny domes
They contain your chromosomes
And the tail can kick just like a leg.
O nothing could be finer
Than to swim up a vagina
And make a rendezvous with an egg.
The sperm has one ambition
And that's to gain admission
To the female reproductive canal
And once he gets in it
He swims a millimeter a minute
Along with forty million of his pals.
The sperm is no boob—
When he smells the fallopian tube
He goes into some crazy figure-eights
About ten thousand times
As those female enzymes
Keep egging him on to penetrate.
A few sperm advance

And do their little dance
And only one gets through the egg membrane
And the merger of those two—
That's what led to you.
So be thankful that your folks did not abstain.

That old man in the garage
Once let loose a great barrage
And though he now is ancient and infirm
And his breath is bad,
Children, he's your dad
Because he contributed those sperm.

You can get them from a bank
Or from Bill or John or Frank
But when it comes to fatherhood there's just one guy to
    thank.
He was young and he was dumb
But when things began to hum
He did not withdraw,
He became your pa,
And that, my dears, is where you all came from.

FIRST TRIMESTER

I feel sick. Nauseous, sweaty, lumpy, queasy.
Others laugh. I'm uneasy.
Had a big lunch I'm about to lose.
I've got the first-trimester blues.

People stare at the little bulge, I know,
And think, My, my, she's let herself go.

I ought to be overjoyed with elation.
I'm thinking about hemorrhoids and constipation.
And I'm so tired I can barely hold a teacup.
And I'm thinking, yup, I'm gonna throw up.

Weird hormones flood my brain.
I laugh, I cry, I feel insane.
Men stare at me. I say, "Hi, mister,
I'm not crazy, I'm in my first trimester."

No pale blush of motherhood here, no bloom.
My little belly has become someone's room.
I feel fat and I used to be elegant, slim.
My husband says I'm beautiful. Screw him.

FORBIDDEN DELIGHTS

Secret tastes, forbidden delights,
Guilty pleasures late at night—
So many things a person wants
Are not found in restaurants.

Such as Chocolate Bacon Cake
At night when no one is awake
And if everyone is truly gone,
Fried eggs slathered with Dijon
And (may I add in parentheses)
A thin slice of Velveeta cheese.
Cheese and Spam in batter, fried,
A pleasure not to be denied.
No, you won't find it in Julia
But Spam is truly a
Treat, in a panini, heated, and which
Combined with Velveeta, makes a good sandwich.
Toasted bread, hot Spam, and two melted slices
Of Velveeta: you feel like Dionysus.
And if you're still hungry, for goodness sake,
There's always Chocolate Bacon Cake.

THE COURSE OF LIFE

If you are in love deep
Or think you might be
And you're about to leap,
Leap carefully.

If the romance starts to fly
And you feel wild and free,
As you rise up to the sky
Rise carefully.

When at last you're man and wife
And happily wed,
And you embark on daily life,
Lose your head.

Daringly,
Be extreme.
Fly to Rome and Normandy.
For breakfast eat ice cream.

When you've been together long,
Your anniversary
Should be marked with feast and song.
Do it gloriously.

Love, long-lasting, on the rise,
Let the water boil.
But don't forget to exercise
And change your motor oil.

MOTHER'S POEM

Some mornings I get up at five.
With four to mother, one to wive,
I find the hours from light to dark
Are not enough to matriarch
With goals for matriarchy high
Among the apples of my eye.

This little girl with golden braid
Expects her toast a certain shade;
Her scrambled eggs must meet the test
Of excellence and gently rest
Upon the toast and not beside.
The little boy wants his eggs fried
Yet not be greasy on his lips,
Accompanied by bacon strips
Fried til they resemble bark.
The older boy takes his toast dark
And if his golden eggs should not
Be poached and served up steaming hot,
Two slightly liquid yellow bumps
Of yolk in solid white, he slumps
Down in his chair and has a mood.
The older girl eats rabbit food,
Berries, nuts, sunflower seeds,
Leaves and stems, and as she feeds,
She is displeased. It's all my fault.
I bought her seeds containing salt.
And worse—some juice containing sugar.
She glares as if I were a crook or,

Worse, a mother short on sense
And guilty of child negligence.
Negligence in the name of love
Is just what we should have more of.
Don't mother birds after some weeks
Of looking at those upturned beaks
Deliberately the food delay,
Hoping to hear their goslings say,
"What are these feathered floppy things
Attached to us? You think they're wings?"

This helpful trusty friendly Frau
Is starting her neglect right now.
The clothes you counted on to leap
Up while you were fast asleep
And wash themselves for you to wear
Have let you down. They just sat there.
The bicycle you thought would pick
Itself up when the rain got thick,
The homework you forgot to do,
Assuming I would tell you to—
My child, you have been betrayed.
The world you thought was neatly made,
Its corners tucked in like a sheet,
Is uncomposed and incomplete.
For years I carried on a hoax.
I made you think that scrambled yolks
Or poached or boiled, fried or shirred,
Are how they come out of the bird.

I made you think that big dustballs
Tiptoe softly down the halls
Out to the trash, that your wool skirt
(The one with emblems of dessert)
Took a cab down to the cleaner,
In answer to a court subpoena.

No matter what you have been told,
The rainbow holds no pot of gold,
Babies aren't found under rocks
Or in Sears Roebuck catalogues,
Those coins weren't put there by an elf—
The Tooth Fairy is me myself,
The Easter Bunny's make-believe,
Cows don't talk on Christmas Eve,
The moon is not made of green cheese,
And eggs don't come the way you please,
Served by hens on silver trays,
And neither does much else these days.

GRADUATION SONG

O here's to the children who grew up too soon,
Who all graduated one morning in June,
Lindsay and Megan and Kevin and Sean—
We kissed them goodbye and bang they were gone.

We're sorry for dumb things we did—
We meant well and we love you, kid.
And as we drive home, your old mother and I
Will think of you fondly and maybe we'll cry.

But after an hour, we've run out of tears.
And we'll look ahead to our post-parent years
When we'll spend your inheritance to the last dime
Having ourselves a remarkable time.

We'll be lovers once more, not cops and chauffeurs.
We'll enjoy all the foods to which you were averse,
Oysters and artichokes and steak tartare,
As we listen to Jerry Garcia's guitar.

We'll throw all our parenting books away.
Farewell to Boy Scouts and the P.T.A.
No more church youth groups, thank God, Amen.
And we'll never watch soccer ever again.

So good luck to you, kid, on your big day.
Hope to see you for Christmas, but if not, okay.
Here's a hundred bucks toward rent and gas,
Now we're off to Paris, flying first class.

5

THANKS BE TO GOD
FOR KEEPING
US SMALL

PUBLICITY

Listen, my children, and you shall hear
Of the midnight ride of Paul Revere,
Who rode along with Sam Prescott
And William Lawes, but Revere got
The nod cause he rhymes with "year,"
So "One if by land and two if by sea"
Was given to Mr. Revere, though he
Was only one rider of the three,
And Sam and Bill gave many alarms
To various Middlesex towns and farms
But wound up in obscurity
Because the names Sam Prescott
And William Lawes simply were not
As pleasant to the poet's ear,
And so we revere one cavalier
And two were denied their rightful fame.
It all comes down to the sound of your name.
If Henry Thoreau had been Wally Ballou,
Would we still esteem *Walden* as we do?
If Emily Dickinson's name had been Misty,
Would she have gotten so much publicity?

So listen, my children, and you shall learn:
Life takes many an unfair turn.
Many a hero goes unsung.
And I will make this simple assertion:
Though you're idealistic, and brave, and young,
Get yourself a publicity person.

HOW TO WRITE A LETTER
TO YOUR MOTHER IN SEVEN DAYS

Day 1: Start a brown rice and broccoli diet, with a small green apple for dessert.

Day 2: Clean your apartment. Stay on your diet.

Day 3: Continue cleaning and dieting and call up your stupid boyfriend and tell him you don't ever want to see him again ever.

Day 4: Look at the Help Wanted ads as you continue cleaning your apartment and dieting and don't pick up when your idiot boyfriend calls. Let him leave pleading messages.

Day 5: Get your hair cut and respond to a Help Wanted ad and continue cleaning and dieting and ignore the boyfriend's pathetic voice mail messages.

Day 6: Go visit Grandpa at the Good Shepherd Home and report for your job interview in the nice navy-blue suit you found while cleaning your apartment which fits you now that you've lost weight and you get the job because your self-esteem is way up now that you ditched the idiot boyfriend.

Day 7: Go to church in the morning and call up Grandpa and write a letter to your mother.

"Dear Mother, Sorry I didn't write sooner. Busy week. Cleaned the apartment (sorry it was a mess when you were here) and looked for a job (think I found one). Only had time to visit Grandpa once but he seems fine. By the way, Tom and I split up. It's difficult but for the best, I know. Got my hair done (picture enclosed). And did I tell you, I've lost three pounds? Love, Wendy."

LUTHERAN STORY

I was a pastor in Minneapolis
Had no time to call my own
A hundred e-mails in my inbox
Spending hours on the phone
Weddings, funerals, and baptisms
Confirmation on Wednesdays
Thursday morning Bible Study
Answer questions about gays
Preach two services on Sunday
Remember names as folks pass by
Hello Karen Carl Anna
Elmer Lucy Gustaf—hi!
A Lutheran pastor going crazy—
And I prayed: Dear God, show mercy
And He has now that He's sent me
Out to Hoboken, New Jersey
A Lutheran pastor in Hoboken
Knows when all is said and done
Catholics in Hoboken
Outnumber us a thousand to one
Now and then someone walks in
With something that they find upsetting
Or to discuss a minor sin
Now and then there is a wedding
I have a coffee break at ten
Lunch at noon
And then take off my shoes,
Close my eyes
And snooze.

It's like being Unitarian in Dallas,
Or a Baptist in Seattle:
A quiet life, free of malice
High above the sectarian battle.
A Lutheran in Hoboken: there's no fuss,
There's 300,000 of them
And a couple hundred of us.
Thanks be to God for keeping us small.
No one notices us at all.
God save us from revival.
We prefer to be archival.
Our church, a secret den
For just us Lutherans. Amen.

FUNDAMENTALIST RAG

We're the elect who are born again,
Trust in the Lord and say Amen.
We give thanks before each meal
And never neck in an automobile.
Before we're 21 we marry
And study to be a missionary.

We are S-a-v-e-d
And take the Bible literally,
Every word and every comma
From Genesis to Jesus' mama
And every prophet and disciple,
It's all true cause it's in the Bible.

On the Lord's Day we don't mow the lawn,
Don't turn the TV on.
We get our thrills from Revelations
And thinking about the Tribulation
When we will rise up in the air
And you agnostics won't be there.

We don't drink liquor or come near it:
The body is the temple of the Holy Spirit.
Don't go to movies or to dances.
Don't go to parties, why take chances?
We flee from sin, especially lust.
Cross your legs. In God we trust.

Lutheran, Episcopalian,
Methodist—are entirely alien.
For Mormons we have no use.
Even Baptists are much too loose.
They don't know what they missed
Not being fundamentalist.

Rock of Ages, cleft for me.
Just as I am without one plea.
I know whom I have believed.
Nearer My God to Thee.
Crown Him with many crowns.
Amazing Grace, how sweet the sound.

LUTHERANISM EXPLAINED

I was raised in Iowa, went to St. Olaf,
Norwegian, I'm proud to say.
Thirty years a member of Zion Lutheran,
I'm there every Sunday.
Always sit in the back of the church,
Always in the same pew.
I like the folks who sit back there,
They're Norwegian too.

We are a modest people
And we never make a fuss
And it sure would be a better world
If they were all as modest as us.
We sing the hymns, listen to the sermon,
Go up front and commune,
Drop in the money, shake hands with the pastor
And we're out by a quarter to noon.

Episcopalians are proud of their faith,
You ought to hear them talk.
Who they got? They got Henry the 8th
And we got J. S. Bach.
Henry the 8th'd marry a woman
And then her head would drop.
J. S. Bach had 23 kids
Cause his organ had no stop.

We got a female associate pastor
And she's nice, don't get me wrong,
But the boots she wears are what I'd call sexy
And the skirt's not what I'd call long.
She's single and she smiles a lot
And she sure does like her beer
And I've been talking to some of the others
And we trust she's gone next year.

Here at Zion Lutheran
Attendance seems to be down
And that's because most of the membership
Is six feet underground.
We don't go for long-term planning,
No need to look that far.
Luther said we're saved by grace
So we're good enough just as we are.

If you come to church, don't expect to be hugged,
Don't expect your hand to be shook.
If we need to know who the heck you are,
We can look in the visitors book.
I was raised to keep a lid on it,
Guard what you say or do.
A Mighty Fortress is our God
So He must be Lutheran too.

REDEMPTION

Jimmy worked at Goldman Sachs
Helping tycoons and nabobs
Avoid paying income tax
So they could create jobs.
Louis XIV and Marie
Antoinette, Lord Elgin,
The Marquis of Queensberry,
And Prince Leopold of Belgium
Were his clients,
And various czars and shahs
And it wasn't exactly rocket science
Avoiding the tax laws.

But one morning he arrived at Sachs
In his long black limousine
And saw a peasant with an ax
Standing by a guillotine.
Angry rumbles, scary talk,
Mobs of peasants on the scene.
He told his chauffeur: "Round the block
And stop the limousine"
And he who had been a creature
Of Wall Street, took off his suit,
Put on jeans and T-shirt
And became a recruit
Of the revolution.
He held Marie's little hand
As she lay her head in the notch,

He gave the command,
And the blade went *sssssssswotch*
And stopped
And her little head dropped
Into the basket. Then he sold
Locks of her hair for silver and gold
And paid his fare
To St. Paul and settled there
And changed his name
To Ernest and became
A progressive Democrat.
And that was that,
That's all he wrote.
He turned his coat
And became a winner.
Today's sinner
Is tomorrow's best friend.
The End.

SOCIAL MOBILITY

On Sunday let us take a ride
From our little apartment on the West Side
Of Chicago and up to the North Side go
To see where we'll live when we get the dough.

When our stock hits 50 and 55
We'll buy a place on Lake Shore Drive.

And when the stock goes through the ceiling
We'll move to Deerfield or maybe Wheeling
And jack up the stock with a mountain of debt
And buy a Northbrook mansionette.

As the bubble inflates like in the '80s
We'll move to Winnetka and buy a Mercedes
And a stone castle in Lake Forest
And then I suppose we'll get divorced.

You'll get the house, I'll get what remains,
And buy a condo in Des Plaines,
And a 1990 Honda
And date a faded blonde named Rhonda.

When the company tanks, I pray to God
That when I am indicted for fraud
The jury acquits and I don't get
A furnished cell in Joliet.

SONG OF OCTOBER 12

Columbus sailed the ocean blue
Back in 1492.
He sailed across and spotted land,
A beach, and people on the sand.

He called them Indians because
He had no idea where he was,
India was just a guess.
When in doubt, declare success.

Calling this Columbus Day
As if he'd found the U.S.A.,
You may as well say you're Gershwin
Because you whistled, "Love Walked In."
Or drop an apple and start tootin'
Your horn as if you were Isaac Newton.

Everybody knows the one
Who got here first was Leif Eriksson.
He sailed to Newfoundland, Cape Cod,
And did not come in the name of God
To steal the gold and claim the land
And evangelize the native band
And kill them off with smallpox.
He picked some apples, went for walks,
Traded knives for moccasins,

Sat down and wrote his sagas in
Old Norse and sailed to Oslo
And saw a friend and told him, "Ja so
I just got back from way out west."
And the friend said, "Oh ja. I sorta guessed
You were gone. Where'd you go?"
"Oh, off to the New World, don't you know."
He could've proclaimed the whole of
America belonged to King Olaf,
But instead he shrugged and said, "Hey!
Let October 12th be Columbus Day.
Whatever. I am totally okay
With that. Hip hip hooray!"
And he continued seafaring
Back home for a plate of herring
And a glass of beer to quench his thirst.
He knew he got there first
Or, as Columbus might say, *a priori,*
And as people heard the story
Eventually he'd get the glory.

UNSPOKEN PRAYER

You just wait until next year.
Justice will be done.
You'll be crying in the cellar
And we'll be number one.
Enjoy the interviews,
Your awards banquets.
Next year when you lose
You'll be sucking on regrets.
Next year we'll be singing
As we're showered with champagne,
We'll be riding in a limo
And you'll be walking in the rain.
We'll be on the covers
Of glossy magazines
And you'll be scrounging in your cupboard
For a can of navy beans.
The high shall be brought low,
That's what Scripture says.
The Lord is going to show
You some real unhappiness.
That is what I pray for,
That is a loser's prayer.
Jesus is my savior
And He'll lift me high up there
To the heights of glory
And cover you with shame.
I don't say it Sunday morning
But I think it just the same.

JIM FLAM STEPS ASIDE

I would like to express my thanks
To my faithful volunteers
Who worked so hard all year,
Raising money, going door to door, manning the phone
  banks.
You've been such an inspiration to me,
And thank you from the entire Flam family
For all you've meant
In my race for President.
All of you have been absolutely great.
But I have decided I can no longer be your candidate.
(SHOUTS OF "NO, NO")
It was one of the best-run campaigns I ever saw,
But I have decided to withdraw.
(SHOUTS OF "NO, NO")

I am not bitter. I don't blame the press for how I was
  treated.
Sometimes you win, and sometimes you have to go out
  there and eat it.
I feel like the luckiest man in America today,
And that's because of this lady here: and I refer to Kay.
(APPLAUSE)
Thirty years we've been married, and that's a while:
But she's always at my side, looking up with a smile.
Isn't she great? I couldn't be prouder.
I couldn't have done it without her.
(APPLAUSE)

I am a survivor. That's the kind of guy I am.
So don't worry for a minute about Jim Flam.
I want to make one thing clear today
As I go away.
I still have $3,000,000 in my campaign treasury,
And federal law says that at a candidate's pleasure he
Can use that money for any goldarn thing he wants
And so I am moving to a villa in Provence,
On the Riviera,
And not with Kay but with Sarah,
One of my volunteers,
And though the age difference of forty-one years
May seem scandalous,
It feels just right to us.
(SILENCE)
On those miserable campaign days
In dingy Iowa cafés
Shaking hands
As if you stand a chance,
But people are avoiding you
And polls show you dropping from four to two
Percent, and your speech is a wheel without spokes:
People are laughing at your applause lines and clapping
    for the jokes.
In short, you have entered political hell
Except for 11 p.m. in the hotel
When you take the elevator up to the fifth floor,
To room 504, and knock on the door,

And it opens and there a
Vision of beauty, Sarah,
Stands in her pale pink lingerie,
And all your sorrows fade away
And your interest in policy and the difference you can
    make and how you can make it
And you just want to be naked.
(AWESTRUCK SILENCE & WHISPERS)

Thank you for what you've done and who you are.
Au revoir.
To heck with the kids, the oppressed, the hungry, the
    needy.
Let's go, sweetie.

(FOOTSTEPS, DOOR OPENS, CLOSES)

6

SECONDARY NEURONS OF THE CEREBRAL PROMONTORY

BIRTHDAY POEM FOR MOZART

When Mozart was three, he began to play the clavier;
When he was five, he began to compose;
When he was ten, already launched on his career,
He began to worry about his hair and clothes.
"Am I cool?" he wondered. "Is this the wig I should be
    wearing
Or should I have gotten the brunet?
Are these knee britches baggy? Why is everyone
    staring?
I wonder if they'll like my new quartet."
Even a genius is full of doubts
About his looks and the future and melody and rhythm,
And though the audience stands and claps and shouts
Bravo, he wonders if anyone would like to go have a
    drink with him?

He and his wife Constanze were not so astute
When it came to money. No, not them.
So after he'd finished writing *The Magic Flute*
He had to get busy on the *Requiem*.
He had to pay for their extravagances
So his work was never done.
Serenades and German dances
And the Piano Concerto No. 21
To pay for clothes and wine and gelati
And the expense of yet one more infant he
Composed the *Exsultate, Jubilate*
And the *Jupiter* Symphony.

Had he and Mrs. Mozart avoided going in debt
And been cautious and frugal,
He might've written one small motet
And maybe a concerto for bugle.

Thank you, Mozart, for being so prolific
And by the way your hair looks terrific.

BIRTHDAY POEM FOR F.S.F.

Dear Scott Fitzgerald,
You were the herald
Of the Age of Jazz
And of a generation
Of elegant syncopation
And the freedom that true jazz has.

You were born in St. Paul
Which you didn't like at all
And had to go away to feel alive.
You blazed, then you cracked,
You had no second act,
You were perpetually 24 or 25.

Summer, 1919,
You stood between
Failure and great success.
You reached for the prize
This side of Paradise,
And Zelda wrote back and said yes.

You were destiny's child
With a beautiful style
And they couldn't get enough of you
For about ten years
And then your career
Descended and vanished from view.

But straight to the end
Of your awful descent
To that bungalow in L.A.
Through sickness and the blues
You were true to your muse
And aspired to greatness every day.

At age 44
You went through the door,
Leaving a few books behind
That people still read,
That somehow succeed
In tiptoeing into the mind.

Some paragraphs flash
And thunder and crash
And shine on the page. Some do not.
You had troubles, God knows,
But what beautiful prose—
Happy birthday. R.I.P. Thank you, Scott.

ADDRESS TO THE HARVARD
CHAPTER OF PHI BETA KAPPA,
SANDERS THEATRE, JUNE 2008

The ranks of Harvard Phi Beta Kappa orators include
Not many whose careers were made from laughter,
But rather men of intellect and rectitude,
Whom college buildings are named after,
Such as Ralph Waldo Emerson and, many years ago,
    Socrates,
All of them top-notch, no mediocrities,
Who gave speeches of moral weight and literary quality;
Well, this year you are taking a holiday.
For you have added to that distinguished legion,
A minor Midwestern comegion
Who came because, as it happens,
People who become Phi Beta Kappans
Tend to be what one might call dry
And spell comedy c-o-m-i-t-y.
It all started with prenatal math,
The mother reading French declensions in the bath,
The warm water intended to calm the fetus
And maximize the effect of the Bach partitas
Which promote the growth of the secondary
Neurons of the cerebral promontory,
Increasing the residuary
Inventory
Of functionary
Improvisatory
Vocabulary

Authorities consider necessary
To get into a first-rate Montessori.
An advanced Montessori where smarter children are
    created,
Where the sandbox is enriched and naptime
    accelerated,
And every child, Muslim, Buddhist, Jew, or Gentile,
Is targeted for the 99th percentile.

O brave young achievers, you have now achieved the
    pinnacle
And forgive me if it sounds cynical
But as we gather to celebrate ya and hail ya
It is time for you to think about the benefits of failya.
Failure is essential, a form of mortality.
Without failure, we have a poor sense of reality.
It is all well and good to strive for glory,
But today's grievous mistake is tomorrow's humorous
    story.
And one should not be a person whose memoirs consist
Of notes from the classes you never missed.

Would the Prodigal Son's dad have killed the fatted calf
If the boy had graduated with an average of three-
    point-ninety-nine and a half?
No, nor would Job have grown so wise in the Lord's ways
Had his only tribulation been one or two B's among a
    whole long string of A's.

In a nutshell, my advice is:
Go out and have a crisis.

A person who lives a charmed life,
Gets the great job and size 2 wife,
The starter mansion that proclaims
His wealth, the beautiful children with Celtic names.
At the age of forty, a successful stock analyst, he
Will run off with a cocktail waitress named Misty,
Take up cocaine and dungarees and permed hair
And write third-rate poems in the style of Baudelaire
And endure ten years of spiritual emptiness and hunger,
That would've taken two months if he'd done it when
    he was younger.

Don't wait until next week or even tomorrow.
Speak to your parents today, while they're still proud,
    and ask to borrow
Two or three thousand bucks and have yourself a
    beautiful disastrous summer
And not just a boring one but a real bummer.
Go to Paris, St. Petersburg, Machu Picchu,
And learn what Harvard cannot teach you
Whether you get a bachelor's or a master's:
The fact that being a traveler means learning to
    weather disasters.

If you are on a career path toward pediatrician or attorney,
Interrupt it and take a journey
For a month of indolence and occasional dishonor
Among people who don't understand you and don't
even wanna.
Among strange music and voices, foreign sights and
smells,
Sleazy barrooms and city parks and cheap hotels,
The streets thronged with traffic, pedestrian and
vehicular,
And all those exotic people and one in particular
Who stops and talks and you strike up a tête-à-tête
And gradually in the course of an hour become a duet
And you go for a walk along the Seine
And kiss as if you might never kiss again
But then you kiss again and then one thing leads to
another
And you have an experience you won't be sharing with
your mother.

Have a disastrous summer so that as the autumn days
  come nigh
Your misadventures are the talk of other alumni.
Forget about excellence. Think about courage.
And let that audacious side of you emourage.
You are excellent. Even if you were delivering pizza,
I would know you, like when a body meets a
Body coming through the rye, or coming through the
  trees,
You can recognize excellence even if it smells of onions
  and cheese.

And now congratulations on your great success,
Good luck as you head down the corridor.
Thank you for listening to my address.
It was an honor to be your orator.

FOR RAY AND ORRELL ON THEIR 50TH ANNIVERSARY

Of all the great romantic tales
Of ladies bountiful and fair
And handsome and obsessive males,
From Antony and Cleo
To Ginger Rogers & Fred Astaire
In *Flying Down to Rio*—
Of all the tales that could be told,
Both decent and immoral,
Was ever there a love so bold
As when a Raymond met an Orrell?
When, from his bath, the shy young man
Discerned a voice of mystery
Talking with his mother, heard
A Smart Young Thing from Rutherford,
Came down the stairs and thus began
A long romantic history,
Whose griefs were few and joys were many:
Kristina, Elsa, Eric, Jenny.

They courted for a month or more
And then set out to marry,
This Holman from the Jersey Shore,
The Nilsson from the prairie.
Their hearts were light and unafraid,
Not knowing how heroic
It is for a high-strung Yankee maid
To wed a Swedish stoic.

So opposite their natures were,
Their knowledge of each other dim,
He spent five decades studying her,
She spent the same researching him.

And now, on their historic date,
We join in celebration
Of Ray and Orrell Nilsson's great
Ongoing conversation
With each other as a mate
Of endless fascination.

FOR JOHNNY

There was a fiddler named Gimble
Whose fingers were nimble
To play all the licks and the trills.
He could play "Darling Nelly"
Or Stéphane Grappelli
Or tunes that were old as the hills.
He played the "Orange Blossom"
So the people would toss him
Dimes, quarters, and some dollar bills.
He played shows and dances
From Texas to Kansas
With a fiddler by the name of Bob Wills.

And as he got older,
The fiddle on his shoulder
Seemed as natural as a flag on a pole.
He smiled as he played
Some old serenade
And the music came up from his soul.
You could hear the stars falling
And the whip-poor-will calling
Whenever he picked up his bow.
And the shuffling and sliding
Of ghost dancers gliding
On kitchen floors long long ago.

BAKER'S DOZEN

I used to do avant-garde dance
With a blowtorch, blue paint, and no pants,
Which many folks guessed
Was genius, and the rest
Left gladly when given the chance.

A barber who lived in Connecticut,
Regardless of whose patron's head he cut,
Liked to sharpen his shears
And snip off their ears,
A grave violation of etiquette.

A liberal lady of D.C.
By day was tasteful and p.c.
And then after ten
She went out with men
Who were rednecks, vulgar and greasy.
"When it comes to the masculine specie,"
She said, "Believe me, I'm easy,
But liberal guys
Tend to theologize
And I am not St. Clare of Assisi."

There was an old liberal named Kurt
Who wore his heart on his shirt.
The poor pay of teachers
Or the death of small creatures
Left him shaken and visibly hurt.

There once was a good Democrat
Who was able to talk through his hat.
Such smart things he said
Off the top of his head
Or else out the place where he sat.

Here is to Marcel Proust
Whose novels often are used
To keep a door shut
Or put under the butt
To give a short person a boost.

A Southerner named Roy A. Blount
Had a red gravy stain down his front
When he came to St. Paul
And he spoke with a drawl.
They thought he was drunk but he wun't.

Here's to my friend Ira Glass
Who tends to mumble, alas.
I can't tell by his voice
If he's reading James Joyce,
Speaking Flemish, or saying the Mass.

A sinuous lady named Duke
Leaned languidly against a juke-
Box flashing bright red
And what her eyes said
Is not found in the Gospel of Luke.

A vegan who lives in Seattle
Does not eat fish, fowl, or cattle.
No meat, blood, or bone,
Or greens that were grown
On or nearby a field of battle.

There was an old man quite embittered
By how he had wasted and frittered
His best years away
In listening all day
To reruns of *All Things Considered*.

There was an old singer of Syracuse
Who was startled to hear his dear accuse
Him of losing his marbles
Cause sometimes he garbles
The words that the writers of a lyric use.

A vegan with nothing to do
Picked up a sandwich to chew
And took a big bite
And cried out in fright,
"OMG! WTF! BBQ!"

7

A REPUBLICAN LADY
OF KNOXVILLE

THE OWL AND THE PUSSYCAT

The Owl and the Pussycat fell in love
Though their families told them no.
They rendezvoused in a tender mood
In a grove where the green grass grows.
The Owl looked up to the stars above
And sang to a blues guitar,
"O lovely Kathy O Kathy my love
If only we had a car.
A car.
A car.
If only we had a car."

Pussy said to the Owl, "Your tender avowal
Of love delights my heart.
Let us get carried away and be married,
I'm lonely when we're apart."
Said the Owl, "Let's join our hands in Des Moines
Or Omaha or Butte."
Said the elegant kitty, "How about a city
More romantic, like Duluth?"
Duluth.
Duluth.
More romantic like Duluth.

They left at once and it took them two months
For their car did not run well
But they headed for the great North Shore
And found a swank hotel.
And there in the lobby was a pig named Bobby

A very intelligent creature.
Full of knowledge, he knew theology
And was a Baptist preacher.
A preacher.
A preacher.
He was a Baptist preacher.

"Dear Pig, is it possible to put down the gospel
And marry a cat and a bird?"
Said the pig, "For a dollar I'll put on a collar
And read you from God's Holy Word."
Down by the lake round a big wedding cake
They had them a ceremony.
And recited a verse and for better or worse
They entered matrimony.
They did.
They do.
They entered matrimony.

They looked at Two Harbors but there were no barbers
Who could style feathers and fur.
They looked at Chisholm where Catholicism
Was strong and that's not what they were.
They thought about Ely but found it really
Too wild and somewhat uncouth.
And Grand Marais was too far away
So they settled in Duluth.
Duluth.
Duluth.
So they settled in Duluth.

They promised of course to share household chores
And their names they would hyphenate.
They'd live happily and if children there be
They'd be raised in the Lutheran faith.

They feel elite on Superior Street
Where they live in a telephone booth.
They are odd, I suppose, but no more than most
Who live there in Duluth.
Duluth.
Duluth.
Who live there in Duluth.

THE FOX WENT OUT
ON A CHILLY NIGHT

The Fox went out on a chilly night,
Took a left at the town stoplight,
Thought he'd stop and get a bite
As he drove through the town-o.

He drove up to the Goose drive-in
Which was open late and he looked therein
And he gave the lady a foxy grin
As he rolled his window down-o.

"Gimme a goose, family size,
Drumsticks, breast, and thighs
With extra sauce and a side of fries
All roasted nice and brown-o."

He drove back to his cozy den
And there were his little ones, 8, 9, 10.
His wife said, "Fred, you've done it again—
This is processed food you found-o.

"Processed goose is not for me,
Hate the salt and the calories,
Go find a goose who is running free
And scratching for food on the ground-o."

So the fox got back in his car
And searched for a fresh goose near and far,
A goose who ran free in the yard
And weighed about fifteen pounds-o.

He followed his nose through the tall corn rows
And saw some men in hunting clothes.
They yelled, "Get him! There he goes!"
And they released the hounds-o.

Now they're a vegan fox family,
No more meat, and no dairy,
But sometimes Mr. Fox gets free
And sneaks away into town-o.

He goes around to visit the geese
And he preaches about love and peace
And the geese all watch him carefully
As he asks them to kneel down-o.

A TRAGIC SONG

My friends, have you heard how one Christmas Day,
Three little children wandered away,
Far from the turkey, the tree, and the gifts
They wandered lost across white snowdrifts.
Poor kids in the snow.

They were so cold from the snow and the wind
And at sunset they heard a violin
Played by the blind man in his warm hut.
They knocked on the door but it was locked shut.
Poor kids in the snow.

They pounded and made a hullabaloo
But the old blind man was rather deaf too.
They broke down his door, so desperate were they
And found he belonged to the NRA.
Poor kids in the snow.

ANOTHER TRAGIC SONG

In a tavern way down in the Bowery
A lady was plying her trade
As a waitress and quote entertainer
Unquote and a part-time barmaid.
Her hair it was dyed and her lipstick
Was radioactive red,
And the young fellows jeered at her downfall
Til the bartender stood up and said:

She's a girl who got tired of Christmas,
The dinner that she must produce,
The shopping and cleaning and wrapping
So she chose to be lurid and loose.
There are many women just like her
Who wearied of cooking big meals
And now they are drinking gin liquor
And running around in high heels.
Something snapped as they baked Christmas cookies
Or patiently chopped the mincemeat.
So be kind to your wives and your mothers
Lest you find them one day on the street.

O MY DARLING CLEMENTINE

I met her on the Internet,
A chat room called Hard 2 Get.
Our chat was wild, digitally propelled
We jabbered and we LOLed.

She sent me a jpg,
I sent her back one of me
From back when I weighed 163,
Before I went in for third-degree
Assault and robbery.
Now I weigh 209
But I can lose it by the time
She and I finally meet
When I'm out of jail and on the street.

So I sit here online,
Chatting with my Clementine,
Her picture pasted to my screen.
She's my dream at sweet sixteen.
And if she'll only marry me,
What a virtual love it will be.

NIKOLINA

I fell in love with darling Nikolina,
And we decided to be wed.
But when I asked her dad's permission,
He said, "Please wait til I am dead."

Her mother wept so hard she broke her corset,
Her father reached up for his whiskey jug,
The dog jumped up so brokenhearted,
He had an accident upon the rug.

I said, "Is it because you think I can't support her,
Or is there something wrong I might have done?"
Her father said, "It's that you're Swedish,
I never met one who was that much fun.

"You only work, you never go to parties,
You never tell a joke when it's your turn.
You sit there like a stone and don't say nothing,
I'd rather hang out with a Boston fern."

He said, "You're boring and I just don't get it
What Nikolina ever saw in you."
And so I picked her papa up and kissed him,
"Boring, sir? It isn't true."

I danced a jig while telling jokes and riddles
And juggling knives til they were goggle-eyed
And sang duets from *Rigoletto*—
One man, two voices. They were mystified.

I did backflips. I set off rockets.
And somehow managed to burn down the joint
And everyone leaped out the windows.
"Okay," her father said, "I get the point."

And so I married darling Nikolina.
We bought a house right here in town.
We had a baby who we named Christina
And every night to supper we sit down.

I don't tell jokes these days or juggle;
I am a Swede, I'm not a ham.
All my duets I do with Nikolina.
She loves me just the way I am.

WHOOPITIYIYO CALIFORNIA

I'm just an old cowboy with twigs in my hair
I'm two-thirds alligator and three-quarters bear
And one-half a liar but let it be known
I never told one lie that was not my own.

I came to California for the salt air
And for the mountains, which we don't have back there.
What we have is flatness and cold, goodness knows,
So this is a paradise one would suppose.

I walked in San Francisco in the fog and the mist.
I went out a Lutheran, came back a humanist.
Found a hotel and my spirit rejoiced:
That town may be cold but by gosh it is moist.

I've been up north, near the big redwood trees,
Where the people still live in the late seventies,
It's very alternative, and local, and yes
Everything's natural, especially B.S.

I went through Orange County, full of new building sites.
It has no oranges, just orange warning lights.
The freeways were humming, the streets were abuzz
And it didn't look bad for whatever it was.

I spent a few days seeing L.A.
Where everyone's working on a screenplay
Cabdrivers, waiters, grocery clerks, oh yeah—
You doubt it, just ask, they'll be happy to show ya.

San Diego is peaceful and calm and harmonic
Where the only ice is in your gin and tonic.
It is full of Midwesterners in disguise
But I know who they are by the guilt in their eyes.

CLASS WARFARE

It's time for working people to rise up and defeat
The brokers and the bankers and the media elite
And all the educated bums in paneled office suites
And throw them in the street.

Down with all the East Coast liberal aristocracy,
The lawyers who luxuriate in lubricity,
The lobbyists who swan around in Washington, D.C.
We'll run them up a tree.

Let's reverse the social order—oh wouldn't it be cool:
Down with management and let the secretaries rule.
Let the cleaning ladies sit around the swimming pool,
Send the bosses back to school.

We'll snatch them from their country clubs and luxury
    resorts.
Drive them off the golf course and the shaded tennis
    courts.
We'll march up to first class and grab them by the ear
And drag them to the rear.

And then we'll get the media, those mighty millionaires
Who weave their little fictions sitting on their derrieres;
We'll grab them by their flabby hands and make them
    say their prayers
And kick them down the stairs.

We'll grab hold of Mitt Romney by his shiny satin tie
And get him a job cleaning toilets at the Y
And as for that pretentious solemn midget Rand Paul,
He can clean toilets at the mall.

The 99 percent shall rise up with a roar
And latch onto those wealthy louts and make them
    sweep the floor,
Tax the bejabbers out of them and give it to the poor
And throw them out the door.

NINE MORE

A Republican lady of Knoxville
Bought her brassieres by the boxful
Which she stuffed with corn kernels
And old Wall Street Journals
To keep the fronts of her frocks full.

There was an old man of Oak Ridge
Who cried out, "Son of a bitch.
I got up in the night
And turned on the light
And find I have pissed in the fridge."

A gentleman from Chattanooga
Loved to fix greens with arugu-
La and serve up grits
With smoked truffle bits
And maybe a side of beluga.

A strong-minded woman of Memphis
Liked to holler and yell for emphas-
Is. And, if we choose
She does know the blues
And would be more than glad to sing them f' us.

There once was a mezzo named Horne
Whose voice with such passion was torn,
When she played a theater,
About nine months later,
Dozens of babies were born.

The lovely Miss Totenberg (Nina)
Covers the political arena
With the elegant gloss
Of Diana Ross
And the wisdom of the goddess Athena.

A world-famous cellist named Ma
Played Bach on the musical saw
And encored with "Dixie"
As a lady named Trixie
Danced in a G-string and bra.

There was an old man of Ft. Worth
Who said, "I thank God for my birth,
And the shepherds who came
And whispered my name,
And the angels descending to earth."

It's Advent. Here come the Wise Guys
Who've followed the Star in the skies,
And angels, as well as
All us *fideles*,
And who's in that stable? *Surprise!*

8

THE PLANET
REVOLVING ON
ITS AXIS

WINTER BLUES

I hate to see those autumn leaves come down,
The world turn brown.

Always less time than I thought there would be.
I used to kill time, and now time is chasing me.

Nobody knows the trouble I'm in.
Bad times have just begun to begin.

I feel shaky like I could fall
And it's a long way down for a man this tall.

If I were with you, I'd be happy for sure,
Your smile would be my sunshine cure.

If you don't love me, I will go
To a *pueblito* in Mexico.
Learn Spanish in a year or so.
Learn "La Bamba" and "Tico-Tico."
Make a couple *nuevos amigos*.
And maybe they're not so *magnifico* as you,
But they will do.

OPERA

Why is it that, in Rossini and Verdi,
Entertainment is such a rarity?
Verdi's *Aida*
Goes on for hours.
You need a double margarita
And two whiskey sours,
And a double martini
For Puccini.
Rigoletto: by the time it's through
And Gilda's in the bag, I wish I were too.
Don Pasquale is not so jolly.
Strauss's *Ariadne* is pure monotony.
I sat and yawned through *Pelléas and Mélisande*.
And Benjamin Britten
Wrote the most boring music ever written.
And Mussorgsky was modest, of course,
Because his operas were not Godunov, so they Boris.

The *Ring of the Nibelungs*
With all of those goddesses,
The braids and the bodices—
If they had more feeble lungs,
Brunhilde and her crowd
Wouldn't sing so loud
Like someone's been floggin' her,
Someone like Wagner.

BEETHOVEN

At Orchestra Hall, the pianist played the *Moonlight
    Sonata*
To a crowd that was restless as a whole lotta
Moonlight fell on them,
And they coughed up a lot of phlegm.
In the first twenty rows,
People dressed up in what we used to call Sunday clothes,
And in the balcony jeans and sneakers were in fashion
And T-shirts with sayings about living life with passion,
Like the one about wearing purple when I'm an old lady.
Nerdy Jewish teenagers sat with Bubbie and Zadie.
A mother argued with a daughter who said to her finally,
"If I accept your friend request will you stop annoying
    me?"
And a man tried to impress the woman upon whom he
    was gazing
With a comment about the pianist's excellent phrasing.

YOUR FAULT

Those whole grains you fed them
Contained hormones,
The fruit was full of sugar.
You should have known
Your child could get brain tumors
From that mobile telephone.
Pizza made them schizo,
Red meat made them blue.
Things you did ruined your kid
And shame on you.
You put cheese in your boy's arteries
Like big lumps of glue.
And now in a panic you read that organic
Can be bad, too.
You did what you thought was right,
Served fruit and whole grains both,
And now they find that the two combined
Stunt intellectual growth.
Some fruits stimulate estrogen.
The oatmeal is high in salt.
Oh the wrong you have done to your daughters and
   sons,
And it's all your fault.

ONE THING AFTER ANOTHER

Life is just one thing after another.
If it isn't one thing it's bound to be the other.
If you don't believe me, just ask your mother.
Life is one thing after another.

Wake up in the morning and haul out of bed,
And there on the rug the dog did his business.
Your only clean shirt is this weird striped red
Thing your Aunt Joan gave you for Christmas.

The coffeemaker is leaking, doggone,
And your keys are missing, and you can't find the phone,
And there's garbage strewn all over the lawn,
And now you smell gas and it isn't your own.

The children moved home and must be supported,
The bank just sent you an overdraft warning.
You'd like to go south but you can't afford it
And the boss called and said, Can I see you this morning?

You paid fifty bucks for a pair of bad shoes.
Today is a day of defeat, and despair,
You look at the paper, there's so much bad news.
And probably more of which you're not aware.

Life is just one thing after another.
If it isn't one thing it's bound to be the other.
If you don't believe me, just ask your mother.
Life is one thing after another. And another.

ADVICE

Don't put yourself down.
Mind your p's and q's.
Pick up a penny for good luck.
Never buy cheap shoes.
A stitch in time saves nine.
Pride goeth before a fall.
If you wait until your ducks are all in a row
You'll never do much at all.
It's so much simpler to tell the truth.
Time brings all things to light.
You make a better door than a window.
You may as well do things right.
This too shall pass.
Life is not fair.
Don't talk about what you don't know
And always wear clean underwear.

BACK IN THE DAY

Back in the day, my little daughter,
We didn't pay for bottled water,
Back when Elvis was alive
And coffee didn't cost three ninety-five.
Back then there was no Internet,
Google hadn't been invented yet,
There were no chat rooms to go to—
We just sat around and talked to people we knew.

Back then there were no cell phones.
When you left home, you were left alone.
A man didn't always feel connected he
Didn't walk down the street and get a call from Schenectady.
There were no seat belts, no air bag.
You stood on the front seat next to your dad
As he drove down the highway drinking his beer
Or you sat in his lap and helped him steer.

In school, we had Christmas every year
And sang about the Midnight Clear.
You believed in God or said you did
Unless you were a communist kid.
We made planes from balsa models.
There were no safety caps on aspirin bottles,
Labels didn't warn about safety risks,
And music came on black vinyl discs.

I was autistic back in the day
But I didn't know it so I was okay.
There were no play dates, we just ran wild.
If you cried bloody murder, your mama smiled
And said, "Don't you come bawling to me."
Kids were tough cause we had to be.

Every year we went to the Fair,
Spent five or six dollars there,
Went to see the stock car races,
Dropped pingpong balls in plaster vases.
Saw the fat lady and the Siamese twins
And the Penguin Boy with a set of fins.
And I looked at Dad, and deep in my soul
I could not imagine ever being that old.

I'm not nostalgic, darling dear.
I am happy to be here.
I just thought you ought to know
How it was in the long ago.

INDEPENDENCE DAY

My mama didn't teach me to Dare to Be Me,
She taught me to behave appropriately,
And thanks to Mama I possess
Some knowledge of appropriateness—
Don't be a jerk, do your work, pay attention, cool your
    engine,
Try to think things through,
And do unto others as you would have them do unto you.
And on this 4th of July as we celebrate
What made our country great,
I would like to toast with champagne
People who continue to drive in the right lane
And offer a nice cold beer
To the manager, the CPA, the engineer.
I am theoretically in favor of rebelling—
I also believe in grammar and correct spelling.
And thank you for teaching this to your descendants
Even though it crimps their independence.

DARK SKIES

Dark skies
Looking at me
Nothing but dark skies
Do I see

Dark skies
I look at them
Nothing but dark skies
It's one a.m.

Ever so often the sun goes away
It happens at night, every day
It's just a fact, like death and taxes
The planet revolving on its axis

Blue skies
Are up ahead
Goodnight, my darling
Go to bed